The Complete Poems of San Juan de la Cruz

The

Complete

Poems of

San Juan

de la Cruz

TRANSLATED BY

MARÍA BARANDA

AND

PAUL HOOVER

MILKWEED EDITIONS

Published 2021 by Milkweed Editions
Printed in the United States of America
Cover design by Mary Austin Speaker
21 22 23 24 25   5 4 3 2 1
First Edition

Milkweed Editions, an independent nonprofit publisher, gratefully acknowledges sustaining support from our Board of Directors; the Alan B. Slifka Foundation and its president, Riva Ariella Ritvo-Slifka; the Amazon Literary Partnership; the Ballard Spahr Foundation; *Copper Nickel*; the McKnight Foundation; the National Endowment for the Arts; the National Poetry Series; the Target Foundation; and other generous contributions from foundations, corporations, and individuals. Also, this activity is made possible by the voters of Minnesota through a Minnesota State Arts Board Operating Support grant, thanks to a legislative appropriation from the arts and cultural heritage fund. For a full listing of Milkweed Editions supporters, please visit milkweed.org.

Library of Congress Cataloging-in-Publication Data

Names: John of the Cross, Saint, 1542-1591, author. | Baranda, María, translator. | Hoover, Paul, 1946- translator. | John of the Cross, Saint, 1542-1591. Poems. | John of the Cross, Saint, 1542-1591. Poems. English.
Title: The complete poems of San Juan de la Cruz / translated by María Baranda, Paul Hoover.
Description: First edition. | Minneapolis, Minnesota : Milkweed Editions, 2021. | Bilingual edition in Spanish and English. | Summary: "From celebrated contemporary poets María Baranda and Paul Hoover, an exciting collaborative translation of the canonical poems of San Juan de la Cruz"-- Provided by publisher.
Identifiers: LCCN 2020044368 (print) | LCCN 2020044369 (ebook) | ISBN 9781571314918 (paperback ; acid-free paper) | ISBN 9781571319609 (ebook)

Subjects: LCSH: John of the Cross, Saint, 1542-1591--Translations into English.
Classification: LCC PQ6400.J8 A2 2021 (print) | LCC PQ6400.J8 (ebook) | DDC 861/.3--dc23
LC record available at https://lccn.loc.gov/2020044368
LC ebook record available at https://lccn.loc.gov/2020044369

Milkweed Editions is committed to ecological stewardship. We strive to align our book production practices with this principle, and to reduce the impact of our operations on the environment. We are a member of the Green Press Initiative, a nonprofit coalition of publishers, manufacturers, and authors working to protect the world's endangered forests and conserve natural resources. *The Complete Poems of San Juan de la Cruz* was printed on acid-free 100% postconsumer-waste paper by McNaughton & Gunn.

CONTENTS

San Juan de la Cruz

The Life • 3
The Poetry • 13
Translators' Note • 23

The Complete Poems of San Juan de la Cruz

Noche oscura • 28
Dark Night • 29
Cántico espiritual (redacción del manuscrito de Sanlúcar) • 32
Spiritual Canticle (Sanlúcar manuscript) • 33
Cántico espiritual (redacción del manuscrito de Jaén) • 50
Spiritual Canticle (Jaén manuscript) • 51
Llama de amor viva • 68
Flame of Living Love • 69
Coplas del mismo hechas sobre un éxtasis de alta
    contemplación • 72
Songs Written in an Ecstasy of High Contemplation • 73
Coplas del alma que pena por ver a Dios • 78
Songs of the Soul That Aches to See God • 79
Otras del mismo a lo divino • 84
Other Verses to the Divine • 85
Otras canciones a lo divino de Cristo y el alma • 88
Other Songs to the Divinity of Christ and the Soul • 89
Cantar del alma que se huelga de conocer a Dios por fe • 90
Song of the Soul that Rejoices in the Knowledge of God
    through Faith • 91

CONTENTS

Romances • 94

Romances • 95

    Sobre el Evangelio "In principio erat Verbum"
        acerca de la Santísima Trinidad • 94

    Concerning the Gospel "In the Beginning Was the Verb"
        with Regard to the Holy Trinity • 95

    De la comunicación de las Tres Personas • 98

    Of the Communication of the Three Persons • 99

    De la Creación • 100

    Of the Creation • 101

    Prosigue (—Hágase, pues—dijo el Padre) • 102

    It Continues (—Let it be then—said the Father) • 103

    Prosigue (Con esta buena esperanza) • 108

    It Continues (With this good hope) • 109

    Prosigue (En aquestos y otros ruegos) • 110

    It Continues (In these and other entreaties) • 111

    Prosigue la Encarnación • 112

    The Incarnation Continues • 113

    Prosigue (Entonces llamó a un arcángel) • 116

    It Continues (Then he called an archangel) • 117

    Del Nacimiento • 118

    Of the Birth • 119

Otro del mismo que va por "Super flumina Babilonis" • 122

By the Waters of Babylon • 123

Glosas a lo divino (Sin arrimo y con arrimo) • 128

Glosses on the Divine (With and without support) • 129

Glosa a lo divino del mismo autor (Por toda la hermosura) • 132

Gloss on the Divine (For all that's beautiful) • 133

Del Verbo divino • 138

Of the Divine Verb • 139

CONTENTS

Suma de la perfección • 140
The Sum of Perfection • 141
Monte de perfección • 142
The Mount of Perfection • 143

Acknowledgments • 145

San Juan de la Cruz

The Life

→>-<←

One of the great poets of world history for the beauty and mystical spirituality of poems like "Dark Night" and "Spiritual Canticle," which controversially depict the bond between God, the Soul, and the Church in terms of the marriage of a Husband and Wife, San Juan de la Cruz was born as Juan de Yepes y Álvarez in 1542 at Fontiveros, near Ávila, Spain. His father, Gonzalo de Yepes, was brought up in Toledo by his uncles, prosperous silk merchants, following the death of both of his parents. The extended family was prosperous and some of its members had served in high ecclesiastical office. While on a business trip through Fontiveros, however, Gonzalo fell in love with a young woman, Catalina Álvarez, whose impoverished family worked as weavers. Cut off by his uncles for marrying below his station, he found himself with no money or support, and began to work as a weaver. Twelve years later, he died of an illness and left his wife impoverished and in the care of their three sons.

Catalina's skill was to weave *burato*, a blend of fine silk and cotton to be purchased by the wealthy. But the market was bad and business was poor. Unable to care for all of her children, she sent Juan to live in an orphanage, where he was taught to read and write. Apprenticed successively to a carpenter, woodcutter, and printer, he proved incapable of the manual crafts and was sent to work, at the age of ten, in the sacristy of a convent in Medina del Campo. This led to a humble position collecting alms for a hospital that specialized in the free treatment of syphilis for the poor. The staff at the hospital made note of his skills at reading and sent him to a Jesuit grammar school (*colegio*), where, with forty others, he studied Latin, including the works of the masters, Virgil, Horace, and Seneca. He was now on his way to the life of study, worship, and contemplation that was his true calling. However, when offered the chance to prepare for the priesthood, he slipped out of the hospital one night and pledged himself instead to the Carmelite priory of Santa Ana. This "escape" foreshadows a scene in his poem "Dark Night," in which the Soul escapes to "the one who burns in my heart" by means of a "secret ladder," as well as his own escape from a Carmelite priory where he was held prisoner in 1578. Taken into the Order of the Blessed Virgin at age twenty-one, Juan took the name of Fray Juan de San Matias. Hoping soon to be ordained, on the strength of his Latin he was accepted to the University of Salamanca, then one of the leading places of study in Europe, and housed in a very small Carmelite college of the larger institution.[1]

It happened that the mystical poet and thinker Fray Luis de León was in residence at Salamanca at the time. Outspoken, Fray Luis was later to spend five years in an ecclesiastical dungeon for daring to translate the Song of Songs directly from Hebrew into Spanish.[2] The Song of Songs would also prove critical to the poetry of San Juan de la Cruz; likewise, it led to his imprisonment and torture. There is no evidence that Juan, twelve years

---

1 Gerald Brenan, *St. John of the Cross: His Life and Poetry* (Cambridge: Cambridge University Press, 1973), 5-6.

2 Brenan, 7

younger than Fray Luis, studied with the great poet directly. But it would seem likely that Fray Luis influenced his later decision to adopt the Song of Songs as the basis of his devotional poetry.

While studying at Salamanca, Juan displayed a strict devotion to the teachings of the early fathers, as well as mystical theology of Dionysius the Areopagite and Boethius' *Consolation of Philosophy*. His leaning was toward Occam and St. Bonaventura, who were favored by the Carmelites, rather than the university's emphasis on Aristotle, Aquinas, and St. Augustine.[3] Juan fasted with great discipline and would whip his shoulders to the point of bleeding. He was admired for his devotion and studiousness, but he was not well-liked because he refused to participate in small talk with fellow students. He would chastise others for the laxness of their spiritual practice, even at times his superiors.

After his ordination, Juan returned to his home in Medina to conduct his first Mass in the presence of his mother. It happened that Teresa de Jesús, later to become Santa Teresa of Ávila, was in Medina at the time, in the process of establishing reformed Carmelite convents. A mystical poet and spiritual leader of great importance, she persuaded him to join her movement, which emphasized the ascetic and mystical practice that he also favored. In the Discalced (Barefoot) Carmelite practice of Teresa, he found his spiritual home.

Juan became an important part of Teresa's reform. But the course of the reformed Carmelites would not be easy, because their success was resented by the Calced Carmelites in power. To lessen her influence, authorities moved Teresa to the convent at Ávila, where she had previously resided. Nevertheless, with Juan at her

---

3 Brenan, 7

side, she managed to convert the majority of the nuns there to her reformed point of view. When Teresa won the election to serve as Prioress, "the Provincial intervened, excommunicating and cursing the nuns who had voted for the candidate, burned their ballots, declared the election void, and appointed his own candidate."[4] In December 1577, a group of men broke into the house where Juan was living and transported him to a prison at the Carmelite Priory in Toledo. This was not his first experience of imprisonment. The previous year, he had been kidnapped by the Calced Carmelites and held against his will at Medina del Campo, but the papal nuncio, Ormaneto, had intervened. In Toledo, however, Juan was made to live in a locked cabinet in which he could not stand fully erect. His food, consisting of bread, water, and left-over sardines, was given to him on the refectory floor. Following the meal, the monks would strike him with leather whips as they stood in a circle around him. This was a daily occurrence for a time. Later, it was limited to every Friday. The punishment left crippling damage to his shoulders. The cupboard was freezing in the winter and unbearably hot in the summer. One night, however, something miraculous happened. He heard a *villancico*—a popular love song—being sung in the street. The lines were:

> Muérome de amores,
> Carillo, ¿qué haré?
> —¡Que te mueras, alahé!

> I am dying of love,
> Darling, what will I do?
> You should die then, alahé![5]

---

4 Willis Barnstone, *The Poems of Saint John of the Cross* (Bloomington, Indiana: University of Indiana Press, 1968), 12.
5 Brenan, 32

Inspired by the song's lilt and beauty, and given access to pen and paper by a new jailer, Juan wrote numerous stanzas of the pastoral "Cántico espiritual" and the devotional love poem "Noche oscura."

Juan began to plan his escape using a needle, thread, and a pair of scissors the new jailer had given him. While his jailer was on an errand and other friars were taking siesta, he managed to calculate the height of the wall by lowering a small rock tied to the thread. He then calculated that if he cut his rugs into strips and made a rope of them, it would reach within ten feet of the ground. Fray Juan also had to find a way to open the door of his cell. This he managed by gradually loosening, a little each afternoon, the two screws holding the strap and padlock to the door. When the time came, he could pop the screws out with a strong push to the door.

On the day of his escape, in gratitude to his jailer, Juan presented him with the gift of a crucifix that Teresa of Ávila had given him and which he always wore around his neck. On the night he determined to leave, he waited until his jailer was otherwise occupied and fashioned the rope. Gathering all that he needed, he then shoved the door, causing the padlock and strap to fall to the floor. This briefly awakened a visiting provincial and two friars in his company who were sleeping nearby, but they soon went back to sleep. Finding the place along the wall he had selected for the task, he tied the rope to an iron lamp and braced the lamp securely. After removing his habit and tossing it over the wall, he descended quickly and leaped to the ground, landing only a couple of feet from a cliff overlooking the swift moving Tagus. Donning his habit once more, he found a way down to the neighboring courtyard of the Franciscan Sisters of the Immaculate Conception. Unfortunately, the courtyard had no easy means of escape. He risked being trapped there until morning, when he would easily be discovered. After some effort and despite his poor physical condition, he was finally able to climb the low part of the wall by wedging his feet into cracks at a corner. On the street, he passed several people, including a tavern owner who thought he'd been locked out of his lodgings. Eventually he was able to find his way to a Carmelite convent that was friendly to his views. Juan was poorly dressed, having no cape or hood, and his habit was worn and dirty. His health was poor. He could barely stand and spoke in a whisper. Nevertheless, he was warmly greeted by the nuns and given a serving of pears steeped in cinnamon.[6]

Seeing that he had escaped and thinking correctly that he might be found at a Discalced Carmelite location, two friars soon arrived with constables. They searched the outer part of the property but did not insist on entering the cloister, which was forbidden to men. After they were gone, Fray Juan was led into the chapel, where he dictated some verses he had written in prison. Sitting in the choir in long black veils, the nuns listened attentively. According to Magdalena del Espíritu Santo, who later copied his verses, he carried a notebook out of prison containing stanzas of "Cántico espiritual." They included "Oh, ninfas de Judea," "Que bien sé yo la fonte que mana y corre" and the psalm "Super fluminis Babylonis," popularly known as "By the Waters of Babylon."[7]

As it was not safe for Fray Juan to remain in the chapel, the prioress arranged for him to be taken away by Don Pedro González de Mendoza, a canon of the Cathedral who was friendly to the reform movement. After disguising Juan as a

---

6 Brenan, 37
7 Brenan, 38

priest, he took him away in a coach to the nearby Hospital de la Cruz, where Don Pedro was administrator. He was soon further removed to El Calvario, a hermitage in Andalucía, where he spent six months in productive seclusion, completing all but the final stanzas of "The Spiritual Canticle." It was here, while serving as vicar, that he began his commentary, *The Ascent of Mount Carmel*, written for the nuns to justify the symbolism and themes of "Dark Night."

Safe from the Calced authorities, Juan became an official of Teresa's movement. In 1579, at age thirty-seven, he founded a college of the Carmelite Reform at Baeza. He also resided at Baeza as rector of the college until 1582, from which he would often visit his favorite convent at Beas. At this time and during a later residence at Los Mártires in Granada, he wrote the final stanzas of "The Spiritual Canticle" and completed *The Ascent of Mount Carmel*. Eventually two versions of "Spiritual Canticle" came to exist, the Sanlúcar and Jaén.

For most of the rest of his life, he served as prior, provincial, or vicar in locations throughout Spain, including Segovia, Valladolid, and Madrid. As vicar-provincial for all of Andalucía, he traveled through the south of Spain on a donkey in order to visit Reform locations. Trouble began, however, following the death of Teresa in 1582 and the election of Nicolás Doria as the provincial of the Reform, replacing Teresa and Juan's protector, Jerónimo Gracián. Teresa's successor, Ana de Jesús, to whom Juan had dedicated "The Spiritual Canticle," was imprisoned and other followers were assigned to distant posts. When Juan tried to intercede on behalf of Ana de Jesús, he was stripped of his authority and exiled to the Andalucían desert town of La Peñuela, known to be the worst Carmelite location in all of Spain. Fearful of being associated with Fray Juan's poetry, the nuns at Beas destroyed what manuscripts of his they possessed.

In June 1591, the Madrid Chapter-General removed Juan from his office and ordered him to be relocated to Mexico. But this order was rescinded before it could be carried out.

In September 1591, while living at La Peñuela, he contracted a fever and was removed to Úbeda, where the person in authority, once junior to Juan at another Discalced site, came to taunt him every day in his room and refused him comforts offered to others. This man, Fray Francisco Crisóstomo, "was a harsh and rigid man who felt a special antipathy for those who were regarded as saints."[8] Also present to offer reprimands was Fray Diego Evangelista, who had been assigned by Doria to investigate Juan at every turn. This included forcing a false confession by a nun at Beas that Juan had kissed her through the grate of her window. It was at Úbeda that Juan died of tumors and fever on December 14. On his deathbed, he requested that fellow friars read aloud some verses from the Song of Songs. When the church clock struck midnight, Juan spoke his last words, "Tonight I shall sing matins in Heaven." [9]

Remarkable events immediately followed the death of Fray Juan. Because he was believed by many to be a saint, local relic seekers quickly filed into his small room. The relics included his clothes and bandages. Before it could be prevented, one person bit off his toe. Others took fingernails and clippings of his hair. Soon a patron of the priory at Segovia, Ana de Peñalosa, took legal action to acquire the body. Nine months after Juan's death, after midnight, his body was removed from its grave. The corpse had not decayed and gave off a sweet smell, certain

---

8 Brenan, 78
9 Brenan, 81

evidence of Juan's sainthood. The body arrived in Segovia minus some fingers, an arm, and a foot. Despite the further dismemberment and distribution of the body to other priories with claims, the face remained recognizable.[10]

The enemies of Teresa and Juan, Nicolás Doria and Diego Evangelista, died two weeks apart in 1594. In the same year, Elías de San Martin, who was friendly to the Reform teachings of Teresa and Juan, took up Doria's former post as general of the Discalced Carmelites, which had been made into a separate order the previous year by Pope Clement VIII.

In 1726, Juan de la Cruz was canonized by Pope Benedict XIII.[11]

---

10 Brenan, 82-83
11 Brenan, 230

The Poetry

-->->-<-<-

The purpose of San Juan de la Cruz's poetry was devotional, and he did not set out to achieve fame as a poet. However, his adoption of the erotic Song of Songs in order to express the bond between God and the Soul in "Dark Night" and "The Spiritual Canticle" created a poetry of spiritual daring and, ultimately, great popularity. It is easy to see why his themes were viewed as scandalous by conservative forces within the Church. Even his favorite nuns at Beas were concerned about the nature of the analogy. To clarify his message for them, he produced extensive commentaries, with line by line exegesis, for both works.

The Ascent of Mount Carmel, a four-hundred-page prose work explicating "Dark Night," begins: "All the doctrine whereof I intend to treat in this *Ascent of Mount Carmel* is included in the following stanzas, and in them is also described the manner of ascending to the summit of the Mount, which is the high estate of perfection which we here call union of the soul with God."[12] The first forty pages alone are an examination of the poem's opening phrase, "On a dark night." Its "Argument" begins:

We may say that there are three reasons for which this

---

12 *The Complete Works of Saint John of the Cross: Doctor of the Church*. Vol. 1, Revised new edition. E. Allison Peers, ed., trans. (Westminster, MD: The Newman Press, 1953), 9.

journey made by the soul to union with God is called
night. The first has to do with the point from which the
soul goes forth, for it has gradually to deprive itself of
desire for all the worldly things it possessed, by de-
nying them to itself; the which denial and deprivation
are, as it were, night to all the senses of man. The sec-
ond reason has to do with the mean, or the road along
which the soul must travel to this union—that is, faith,
which is likewise as dark at night to the understanding.
The third has to do with the point to which it travels—
namely, God, Who, equally, is dark night to the soul
in this life. These three nights must pass through the
soul—or, rather, the soul must pass through them—in
order that it may come to Divine union with God.[13]

In the biblical Song of Songs, the singer, a young woman whose
skin is dark from working in the vineyards, goes in search of
her lover while others are sleeping:

> Upon my bed by night
> I sought him whom my soul loves;
> I sought him but found him not;
> I called him, but he gave no answer
> "I will arise now and go about the city,
> in the streets and the squares;
> I will seek him whom my soul loves."[14]

In "Dark Night," San Juan gives us a similar search for the
beloved, described in an epigraph as "Songs of the Soul in its
pleasure at having reached the high state of perfection, which

13 Peers, 19-20
14 Song of Sol. 3:1-2 Revised Standard Version

is the union with God, on the path of spiritual denial." The opening stanzas are:

On a dark night,
anxious, by love inflamed,
oh, what good fortune!
I left without being noticed,
my house already at rest.

In the dark, and secure,
disguised by a secret ladder,
oh, what good fortune!,
dark and hidden,
my house already at rest.

In the blissful night,
In secret, where no one could see me,
Nor could I see a thing,
With neither light nor guide,
Except the one who burned in my heart.

That is what guided me
More truly than the light of noon,
Where he awaited me,
The one who knew me well,
Where there seemed to be no one.

Oh, night you guide me!
oh night kinder than the dawn!,
oh night that joined
Beloved with beloved,
beloved in the Beloved transformed!

* * *

San Juan was not the first to employ the Song of Songs in this way. According to Colin Thompson, the philosopher Origen (185-254 CE) "was the first writer to interpret the union symbolized in the Song of Songs between Bride and Bridegroom as between the Word of God (the Logos) and the individual soul—an interpretation that was to become immensely influential."[15]

The lay theologian and philosopher Ramon Llull (1232-1316), who wrote in Catalan, Latin, and Arabic, produced "The Book of the Lover and Beloved" as part of his *Book of Blanquerna*, 1283. Written by his fictional character, Blanquerna, a pope who later becomes a hermit, "The Book of the Lover and the Beloved" consists of 366 paragraphs, or "moral metaphors," designed for daily meditation. It is introduced in Chapter 100 of *The Book of Blanquerna*:

> Blanquerna sat praying and considered the way in which he contemplated God and His Virtues and when he finished his prayer, he wrote down how he contemplated God; he did this every day, varying his prayer with new ideas in order to create many different kinds in The Book of the Lover and the Beloved, so that these would be short and the soul could discourse through many in a short time...

> 1. The Lover asked his Beloved if there was anything left in him to love. The Beloved replied: "Whatever makes the love of a Lover grow remains to be loved in me."

---

15 Colin Thompson. *The Poet and the Mystic: A Study of the Cántico Espiritual of San Juan de la Cruz* (Oxford: Oxford University Press, 1977), 12.

2. The roads where the Lover seeks his Beloved are long and dangerous, crowded with cares, longing sighs, and weeping, but illuminated with love.

3. Many Lovers joined together to love one Beloved, who filled them all with love. Each one carried his Beloved fully in his heart, with gratifying anxiety, and felt a pleasant tribulation from this.

4. The Lover wept and asked: "When will darkness end in the world, so that the roads to hell will close? Or the water that usually runs down, will have the power to rise up? Or the innocent, when will they outnumber the guilty?"[16]

According to biographer Gerald Brenan, an important influence on San Juan's poetry was Garcilaso de la Vega (1501-1536), who introduced the Italian Renaissance style to Spain. He also wrote beautiful, melancholic love poems. The poems of San Juan thus influenced were "Dark Night," "Flame of Living Love," and, for its use of the pastoral eclogue, "The Spiritual Canticle."[17] The form of the *villancico*, or popular ballad, can be seen in San Juan's "Song of the Soul":

How well I know the fountain that springs forth and flows,
even though it is night.

That eternal fountain is hidden,
how well I know where it has its home,
even though it is night.

---

16 *The Book of the Lover and the Beloved*, Mark Johnson, ed., trans. (Liverpool: Aris & Phillips, 1995), 5-7.
17 Brenan, 107-108

> I don't know its origin, because it has none,
> but I know every origin comes from it,
> *even though it is night.*

Brenan also credits a minor religious poet, Sebastián de Córdoba, with making "a pastiche of Garcilaso in which the love poetry of his eclogues and *Canciones* is turned line by line into a religious allegory of the love of God for the soul." Córdoba's book appeared in 1575, and Fray Juan is known to have read it.[18]

Teresa of Ávila may be credited with similar poetic themes. In her poem, "¡Cuán triste es, Dios mio...!" she presents God as a sadly longed-for absent lover:

> Dark is this existence;
> Bitter is its thrall:
> Life that's lived without Thee
> Is not life at all.
>
> Oh, my sweetest Lover,
> Miserable am I,
> *And my yearning for Thee*
> *Makes me long to die.*[19]

Both Teresa and Juan made use of the mystical refrain, "Muero porque no muero," which translates as, "I die because I don't die," in their poems. It appears in Teresa's "Vivo sin vivir en mi..." and Juan's "Coplas del alma que pena por ver a Dios." Teresa and Juan also shared *converso* histories; their families had escaped the Inquisition by converting from Judaism to Christianity. Influenced by the *Alumbrados*, or Illuminati, they

---

18 Brenan, 107

19 *The Complete Works of Santa Teresa of Jesus*, Vol. III, E. Allison Peers, ed., trans. (London: Sheed & Ward, 1946), 285.

believed in mental prayer, a practice opposed by the Church because it put away fear in favor of optimism and "good tidings."[20] Private prayer also denies the validity of a professional priesthood. The *Alumbrados* were among the first to be prosecuted by the Inquisition, beginning in 1524. It was an Illuminist volume, *Tercer Abecedario Espiritual*, by Fray Francisco de Osuna, that inspired Teresa as a girl of twenty to pursue a devotional career.[21]

As mystics, Teresa and Juan were attracted to paradox, especially in relation to the dialectic of absence and presence, darkness and light, knowing and unknowing. True knowledge derives from unknowing; that is, the fruitful acceptance of uncertainty. The same theme joins Keats' concept of "Negative Capability"[22] with postmodern indeterminacy. Unwilling to offer a conclusion, the poet seeks truth by remaining *in process*, forever in the midst of the dialectic. Likewise, in Mallarmé's "Un coup de dés," silence and hesitation are positive values. In the words of Friedrich Hölderlin, "In the rhythmic sequence wherein *transport* presents itself, there becomes necessary *what in poetic meter is called cesura*, the pure word, the counter-rhythmic rupture."[23] Silence as the pure word is a mystical concept.

---

20 Brenan, 97

21 Brenan, 96

22 John Keats, Letter 45, To George and Tom Keats, 21, 27 [?] 1817: "I had not a dispute but a disquisition with Dilke, on various subjects; several things dovetailed in my mind, & at once it struck me, what went to form a Man of Achievement especially in Literature & which Shakespeare possessed so enormously—I mean *Negative Capability*, that is when man is capable of being in uncertainties, Mysteries, doubts, without any irritable reaching after fact & reason—Coleridge, for instance, would let go by a fine isolated verisimilitude caught from the Penetralium of mystery, from being incapable of remaining content with half knowledge."

23 "Remarks on 'Oedipus,'" in *Friedrich Hölderlin: Essays and Letters on*

For San Juan, nothingness was a motive force because it approaches the source. The final work in this volume, "The Mount of Perfection," rightly has the final word on being and non-being:

> To come to the all in all,
> abandon the all in all.
> And when you come to have everything,
> have it with nothing to have.

Written in ABCB ballad stanzas, the romances of San Juan tend to receive less attention than "Dark Night" and "The Spiritual Canticle." But cumulatively they offer an important allegory of the Trinity as a family of three, *Padre*, *Madre*, and *Hijo*. To establish the richness of San Juan's rhymes, here are two stanzas in Spanish:

> En el principio moraba
> el Verbo, y en Dios vivía,
> en quien su felicidad
> infinita poseía.

> El mismo Verbo Dios era,
> que el principio se decía.
> Él moraba en el principio,
> y principio no tenía.

We have translated these lines—indeed, all of the *poesías*—without straining to meet the rhyme. This is an obvious, but necessary loss, in order to maintain the clarity of the theological paradox, as well as that of expression:

Theory, Thomas Pfau, ed., trans. (New York: State University of New York Press, 1988), 102.

In the beginning resided
the Verb, and it lived in God,
in whom it possessed
its infinite happiness.

God was the Verb itself,
the beginning was spoken.
It lived in the beginning,
and it had no beginning.

We are accustomed to the mystery of God as the Word. By
using the word "Verb," however, San Juan presents a far more
active theology. The creation was *spoken* into being. God does
not simply exist. He, She, and It are the pure *predicate* of being.

It was the beginning itself;
that is why it lacked it;
the Verb was called Son,
born from the beginning.

It had always been conceived,
and always it conceived;
it gave its substance always
and always it possessed it.

And so, the glory of the Son
is what was in the Father,
and all his glory the Father
possessed in the Son.

Like the beloved in the lover
one resided in the other,

and this love that joins them
coincided with the same.

    With the one and with the other
in equality and worth;
three Persons and one Beloved,
the sum of them was three.

This is far beyond clever wordplay or metaphysical comedy.
Advanced as theology, it teases out and models the ineffable:
    This being is each one,
and this one only joined them
in an ineffable knot
that to say was not to know.

    By which was infinite
the love that joined them,
because three have only one love,
whose essence was spoken;
for the love, the more it was one,
the more love it created.

To say is not to know. Perhaps this explains why some poetry
is so difficult to bear. Having fallen too far from the ineffable,
it forgets how to whisper and becomes just words. Reading the
romances of San Juan, we encounter complexity but one very
closely focused on the essential. It's wonderful to realize that,
because his philosophical stanzas scan and rhyme so perfectly
in Spanish, they are capable of being sung in the street.

—PAUL HOOVER
March 26, 2016

Translators' Note

-->- -<-

In every generation, it's useful—and even necessary—to have a new translation of the poets who have been important to world literature. This explains the recent retranslation of Rimbaud, Dante, Rilke, Celan, Rumi, Hölderlin, and Pessoa, to name just a few. Idioms change with the times, as well as the attitude toward how translation should be managed. Many translators of San Juan de la Cruz into English have selected to maintain his rhyme, which is sumptuous and persuasive in Spanish. But in doing so, they often disregard the literal meaning of the stanza. Here are the first three stanzas of two other translations of "Cantar del alma," which we have translated under the title "Song of the Soul."

San Juan de la Cruz:

> Que bien sé yo la fonte, que mana y corre:
> aunque es de noche
>
> Aquella eterna fonte está ascondida
> que bien sé yo do tiene su manida
> aunque es de noche.

> Su origen no lo sé, pues no le tiene;
>> mas sé que todo origen della viene,
>> aunque es de noche

Roy Campbell (1951):
> How well I know that fountain's rushing flow
> Although by night

> Its deathless spring is hidden. Even so
> Full well I guess from whence its sources flow
> Though it be night.

> Its origin (since it has none) none knows:
> But that all origin from it arose
> Although by night.

John Nims (1959):
> The spring that brims and ripples oh I know
>> in dark of night.

> Waters that flow forever and a day
> through a lost country—oh I know the way
>> in dark of night.

> Its origin no knowing, for there's none,
> But well I know, from here all sources run
>> in dark of night.

There is no "lost country" in the original Spanish. This is an invention of the translator, and other twists and turns of syntax are created for the sake of the rhyme. The plain sense of the imagery is preferable:

> How well I know the fountain that springs forth and
> flows,
> > *even though it is night.*

> That eternal fountain is hidden,
> how well I know where it has its home,
> > *even though it is night.*

> I don't know its origin, because it has none,
> but I know that every origin comes from it,
> > *even though it is night.*

We present the titles of San Juan's poems as they appear in our source text, *San Juan de la Cruz: Poesía completa y comentarios en prosa*[24]. The title of the first poem in this volume is, in its entirety: "Dark Night: Songs of the Soul in its pleasure at having reached the high state of perfection, which is the union with God, on the path of spiritual denial." The subtitle is significant, because it immediately puts the poem's symbolism into the context of a spiritual search.

We did not include the prose commentaries, because Juan's poetry bears its own inextricable meaning, as seen in the paradoxical lines of "The Mount of Perfection": "To come to possess what you don't possess / go where you don't possess." As poets and readers, we are drawn to the puzzle itself.

Willis Barnstone translated the romances as prose, because he found them "markedly inferior," and felt he "could not make

---

24 Biblioteca La Nación, Editorial Planeta, 2000.

them good poems in English."[25] We would argue that the romances are a necessary part of San Juan's poetry and philosophical system, as extended to the Trinity. In some ways, the romances are more daring as symbology than "Dark Night" and "The Spiritual Canticle," for the *Padre*, *Madre*, and *Hijo* have a complex relationship as Three-in-One:

> You see, Son, that your wife
> was made in your image,
> and insofar as she resembles you,
> with you she will agree;

> but she differs in the flesh,
> that you did not possess in your simple being;
> in those perfect loves
> this law requires

> that the lover resemble
> the one that he desires,
> ·the greater the delight.[26]

Our first draft was produced at María Baranda's residence in Coyoacán, Mexico City, in the years 2010 and 2011. I then worked with it alone, for style in English, at my home in Mill Valley, California. I was fortunate in 2014 to have the assistance of the young poet and scholar Aurelia Cortés Peyron, also of Mexico City, who was my student in the MFA Program in Creative Writing at San Francisco State University.

---

25 Willis Barnstone. *The Poems of St. John of the Cross* (New York: New Directions, 1972), 34.
26 Romance 7, "The Incarnation Continues"

The Complete Poems of
San Juan de la Cruz

Noche Oscura

Canciones del alma que se goza de haber llegado al alto estado de perfección, que es la unión con Dios, por el camino de la negación espiritual

En una noche oscura,
con ansias en amores inflamada,
¡oh dichosa ventura!,
salí sin ser notada,
estando ya mi casa sosegada.

A escuras, y segura,
por la secreta escala disfrazada,
¡oh, dichosa ventura!,
a escuras, y en celada,
estando ya mi casa sosegada.

En la noche dichosa,
en secreto, que nadie me veía,
ni yo miraba cosa,
sin otra luz y guía,
sino la que en el corazón ardía.

Aquesta me guiaba
más cierto que la luz del mediodía,
a donde me esperaba,
quien yo bien me sabía,
en parte donde nadie parecía.

Dark Night

Songs of the Soul in its pleasure at having reached the high state of perfection, which is the union with God, on the path of spiritual denial

On a dark night,
anxious, by love inflamed,
oh, what good fortune!,
I left without being noticed,
my house already at rest.

In the dark, and secure,
disguised by a secret ladder,
oh, what good fortune!,
dark and hidden,
my house already at rest.

In the blissful night,
in secret, where no one could see me,
nor could I see a thing,
with neither light nor guide,
except the one who burned in my heart.

That is what guided me
more truly than the light of noon,
where he awaited me,
the one who knew me well,
where there seemed to be no one.

¡Oh noche, que guiaste!,
¡oh noche amable más que el alborada!,
¡oh noche, que juntaste
Amado con amada,
amada en el Amado transformada!

En mi pecho florido,
que entero para él solo se guardaba,
allí quedó dormido,
y yo le regalaba,
y el ventalle de cedros aire daba.

El aire de la almena,
cuando yo sus cabellos esparcía,
con su mano serena
en mi cuello hería,
y todos mis sentidos suspendía.

Quedéme, y olvidéme,
el rostro recliné sobre el Amado;
cesó todo, y dejéme,
dejando mi cuidado
entre las azucenas olvidado.

Oh night, you guide me!,
oh night kinder than the dawn!,
oh night that joined
Beloved with beloved,
beloved in the Beloved transformed!

On my flowering breast,
reserved only for him,
there he fell asleep,
and I gave him the gift,
and the breeze of the cedars blew.

When I ruffled his hair,
with its serene hand
the air of the battlement
wounded my neck
and all my senses were suspended.

I remained me and forgot me,
I lowered my face to the Beloved;
everything ceased and I left myself,
leaving my cares
forgotten among the lilies.

CÁNTICO ESPIRITUAL

(Redacción del manuscrito de Sanlúcar)

Canciones entre el alma y el esposo

Esposa

¿Adónde te escondiste,
Amado, y me dejaste con gemido?
Como el ciervo huiste,
habiéndome herido;
salí tras ti clamando, y eras ido.

Pastores, los que fuerdes
allá por las majadas al otero,
si por ventura vierdes
aquel que yo más quiero,
decidle que adolezco, peno y muero.

Buscando mis amores
iré por esos montes y riberas;
ni cogeré las flores,
ni temeré las fieras,
y pasaré los fuertes y fronteras.

Pregunta a las criaturas

¡Oh bosques y espesuras,
plantadas por la mano del Amado!
¡Oh prado de verduras,

SPIRITUAL CANTICLE
(Sanlúcar manuscript)

Songs between the soul and the husband

Wife

Where have you gone to hide,
Beloved, leaving me moaning?
Having wounded me,
like the stag you ran away;
clamoring, I followed, and you were gone.

Shepherds, those who ventured there
by the sheepfolds on the hillside,
if by chance you see there
the one I love the most,
tell him I suffer, grieve, and die.

Searching for my loves,
I will go among those mountains and riverbanks,
nor will I pick the flowers,
nor fear the wild beasts,
and I will pass beyond the forts and frontiers.

Question to the creatures

Oh woods and thickets,
planted by the Beloved's hand!
Oh field of greenery,

de flores esmaltado!,
decid si por vosotros ha pasado.

Respuesta de las criaturas

Mil gracias derramando
pasó por estos sotos con presura,
y, yéndolos mirando,
con sola su figura
vestidos los dejó de hermosura.

Esposa

¡Ay!, ¿quién podrá sanarme?
Acaba de entregarte ya de vero;
no quieras enviarme
de hoy más ya mensajero,
que no saben decirme lo que quiero.

Y todos cuantos vagan
de ti me van mil gracias refiriendo,
y todos más me llagan,
y déjame muriendo
un no sé qué que quedan balbuciendo.

Mas, ¿cómo perseveras,
¡oh vida!, no viviendo donde vives,
y haciendo porque mueras
las flechas que recibes
de lo que del Amado en ti concibes?

of enameled flowers!,
tell us if he has passed by.

Response of the creatures

Spreading a thousand graces,
he passed by those groves in haste,
and gazing at them along the way,
with his countenance alone
he left them dressed in beauty.

Wife

Oh! Who will heal me!
From now on, truly,
send no more messengers
who don't know
how to tell me what I desire.

And all those who wander,
offer a thousand of your graces,
which wound me all the more
and leave me dying,
an I don't know what that they keep babbling.

But, how do you persevere,
oh life!, not living where you live,
and living so you will die
of the arrows that you receive,
of what you conceive of the Beloved in you?

¿Por qué, pues, has llagado
aqueste corazón, no le sanaste?
Y pues me le has robado,
¿por qué así le dejaste,
y no tomas el robo que robaste?

Apaga mis enojos,
pues que ninguno basta a deshacellos,
y véante mis ojos,
pues eres lumbre dellos,
y sólo para ti quiero tenellos.

[Descubre tu presencia,
y máteme tu vista y hermosura;
mira que lo dolencia
de amor, que no se cura
sino con las presencia y la figura.]

¡Oh cristalina fuente,
si en esos tus semblantes plateados,
formases de repente
los ojos deseados
que tengo en mis entrañas dibujados!

¡Apártalos, Amado,
que voy de vuelo!

El esposo

Vuélvete, paloma,
que el ciervo vulnerado

Now that you have wounded
this heart, why didn't you heal it?
And because you have stolen it,
why did you leave it behind,
and not keep the thing that you stole?

Extinguish my angers,
for no one has calmed them enough,
and let my eyes see you,
for you are their flame,
it's only for you that I have eyes to see.

[Reveal your presence,
may your sight and beauty kill me;
look, take note, that this ache
of love is never cured,
save by your image and presence.]

Oh crystal fountain,
if on your silver surface,
suddenly you were to fashion
the desired eyes
that I've painted in my heart!

Take them away, Beloved,
soon I must be flying!

Husband

Return, dove,
the wounded stag

por el otero asoma
al aire de tu vuelo, y fresco toma.

La esposa

Mi Amado, las montañas,
los valles solitarios nemorosos,
las ínsulas extrañas,
los ríos sonorosos,
el silbo de los aires amorosos,

la noche sosegada
en par de los levantes de la aurora,
la música callada,
la soledad sonora,
la cena que recrea y enamora.

Nuestro lecho florido,
de cuevas de leones enlazado,
en púrpura tendido,
de paz edificado,
de mil escudos de oro coronado.

A zaga de tu huella,
las jóvenes discurren al camino,
al toque de centella,
al adobado vino,
emisiones de bálsamo divino.

En la interior bodega
de mi Amado bebí, y cuando salía

can be seen from the hillside
refreshed by the breeze of your flight.

Wife

My Beloved, the mountains,
the solitary wooded valleys,
the unfamiliar isles,
the sonorous rivers,
the whispering of the beloved breezes.

The calm night
coupled with the rising of dawn,
the music within silence,
solitude sounded,
the dinner that delights and loves.

Our flowering bed,
embroidered with the caves of lions,
laid out in purple,
built upon peace,
is conferred with a thousand gold shields.

Following in your footsteps,
young women discourse on the path
at the touch of lightning,
at wine's restoration,
emissions of divine balsam.

In the inner wine cellar
I drank of my Beloved, and when I went out

por toda aquesta vega,
ya cosa no sabía,
y el ganado perdí que antes seguía.

Allí me dio su pecho,
allí me enseñó ciencia muy sabrosa,
y yo le di de hecho
a mí, sin dejar cosa;
allí le prometí de ser su esposa.

Mi alma se ha empleado,
y todo mi caudal, en su servicio;
ya no guardo ganado,
ni ya tengo otro oficio,
que ya sólo en amar es mi ejercicio.

Pues ya si en el ejido
de hoy más no fuere vista ni hallada,
diréis que me he perdido,
que andando enamorada,
me hice perdidiza, y fui ganada.

De flores y esmeraldas,
en las frescas mañanas escogidas,
haremos las guirnaldas,
en tu amor florecidas,
y en un cabello mío entretejidas.

En solo aquel cabello
que en mi cuello volar consideraste,
mirástele en mi cuello,

to all of that meadow land
I didn't know a thing,
and I lost the cattle that I used to tend.

There he gave me his breast,
there he taught me a very delicious science,
and in truth I gave him myself,
without keeping a thing;
there I promised to be his wife.

My soul has been possessed,
all of my wealth, in his service;
I no longer watch the cattle,
Nor have any other purpose,
for love alone is my task.

So now, if in the land
I was neither seen nor found today,
you will say that I have been lost,
because, being in love,
I lost myself and I found myself.

On certain special mornings,
we will make our garlands
of emeralds and flowers
that blossomed in your love
and are woven with a strand of my hair.

You looked at the hair
on my neck, only at that strand,
and, meditating on its flight,

y en él preso quedaste,
y en uno de mis ojos te llagaste.

Cuando tú me mirabas,
tu gracia en mí tus ojos imprimían;
por eso me adamabas,
y en eso merecían
los míos adorar lo que en ti vían.

No quieras despreciarme,
que si color moreno en mí hallaste,
ya bien puedes mirarme,
después que me miraste,
que gracia y hermosura en mí dejaste.

Cogednos las raposas,
que está ya florecida nuestra viña,
en tanto que de rosas
hacemos una piña,
y no parezca nadie en la montiña.

Deténte, cierzo muerto;
ven, austro, que recuerdas los amores,
aspira por mi huerto,
y corran sus olores,
y pacerá el Amado entre las flores.

Esposo

Entrado se ha la esposa
en el ameno huerto deseado,

you stood captured by it,
and by one of my eyes you were wounded.

When you gazed at me,
your eyes impressed your grace in me;
because you loved me,
and my eyes deserved
to adore what they saw in you.

Don't despise me,
if you find the dark spot in me,
you can still see in me,
after you have seen me,
that grace and beauty you left in me.

Let's consume the grapes
that have blossomed on our vine;
meanwhile, out of roses
we will make a pine cone,
and no one will be seen on the mountain.

Stop, deathly northern wind,
come, southern wind, that remembers my loves,
breathe in my orchard,
set free its fragrances,
so the Beloved will stroll among flowers.

Husband

The wife has entered
the desired and agreeable orchard,

y a su sabor reposa,
el cuello reclinado
sobre los dulces brazos del Amado.

Debajo del manzano,
allí conmigo fuiste desposada,
allí te di la mano,
y fuiste reparada
donde tu madre fuera violada.

A las aves ligeras,
leones, ciervos, gamos saltadores,
montes, valles, riberas,
aguas, aires, ardores
y miedos de las noches veladores:

Por las amenas liras,
y canto de serenas os conjuro
que cesen vuestras iras
y no toquéis al muro,
porque la esposa duerma más seguro.

Esposa

¡Oh ninfas de Judea!,
en tanto que en las flores y rosales
el ámbar perfumea,
morá en los arrabales,
y no queráis tocar nuestros umbrales.

and she rests as she wishes,
her neck reclining upon
the sweet arms of her Beloved.

Beneath the apple tree,
there you were married with me,
there I gave you my hand,
and you were healed
in the same place your mother was violated.

To the weightless birds,
lions, deer, fallow game,
mountains, valleys, riverbanks,
waters, airs, ardors,
and fears of the nights with eyes:

Through the joyful lyre
and song of serenades I conjured you;
let your angers cease,
and don't touch the wall,
so the wife will sleep more securely.

Wife

Oh young women of Judea!,
while amber sends its perfume
to the flowers and rose bushes,
you dwell in distant places,
and don't want to cross our thresholds.

Escóndete, Carillo,
y mira con tu haz a las montañas,
y no quieras decillo;
mas mira las compañas
de la que va por ínsulas extrañas.

Esposo

La blanca palomica
al arca con el ramo se ha tornado,
y ya la tortolica
al socio deseado
en las riberas verdes ha hallado.

En soledad vivía,
y en soledad ha puesto ya su nido,
y en soledad la guía
a solas su querido,
también en soledad de amor herido.

Esposa

Gocémonos, Amado,
y vámonos a ver en tu hermosura
al monte y al collado,
do mana el agua pura;
entremos más adentro en la espesura.

Y luego a las subidas
cavernas de la piedra nos iremos
que están bien escondidas,

Hide yourself, Dear,
and turn your face to the mountains,
and you don't want to confess;
but you gaze at the companions
of the woman who travels to unfamiliar isles.

Husband

The little white dove
has returned to the ark with a branch,
and now the little turtle-dove
has found her desired mate
in the green riverbanks.

In solitude she lived,
and in solitude she has built her nest,
and in solitude her loved one
guides her alone,
in solitude also, wounded by love.

Wife

Let's take our delight, Beloved,
and go to gaze at your beauty
on the hill and at the heights,
where the pure water flows;
let's enter deeper into the thickets.

And then we will go
to higher caverns of stone
and there we will enter

y allí nos entraremos,
y el mosto de granadas gustaremos.

    Allí me mostrarías
aquello que mi alma pretendía,
y luego me darías
allí tú, vida mía,
aquello que me diste el otro día.

    El aspirar del aire,
el canto de la dulce Filomena,
el soto y su donaire
en la noche serena,
con llama que consume y no da pena.

    Que nadie lo miraba,
Aminadab tampoco parecía,
y el cerco sosegaba,
y la caballería
a vista de las aguas descendía.

the most secret of places,
and delight in the juice of pomegranate.

There you will show me
what my soul desired,
and then you will give me,
there you, my life,
what the other day you gave me.

The breath of the air,
the song of the sweet nightingale,
the grove and its grace
in the serene night,
with flame that consumes and gives no sadness.

And no one looked at it;
nor did Aminadab appear,
and the calm horse ring
and the cavalry
descended within sight of the waters.

CÁNTICO ESPIRITUAL
(Redacción del manuscrito de Jaén)

Canciones entre el alma y el esposo

Esposa

¿Adónde te escondiste,
Amado, y me dejaste con gemido?
Como el ciervo huiste,
habiéndome herido;
salí tras ti clamando, y eras ido.

Pastores, los que fuerdes
allá por las majadas al otero,
si por ventura vierdes
aquel que yo más quiero,
decidle que adolezco, peno y muero.

Buscando mis amores
iré por esos montes y riberas;
ni cogeré las flores,
ni temeré las fieras,
y pasaré los fuertes y fronteras.

Pregunta a las criaturas

¡Oh bosques y espesuras,
plantadas por la mano del Amado!
¡Oh prado de verduras,

SPIRITUAL CANTICLE
(Jaén manuscript)

Songs between the soul and the husband

Wife

Where have you gone to hide,
Beloved, leaving me moaning?
Having wounded me,
like the stag you ran away;
clamoring, I followed, and you were gone.

Shepherds, those who ventured there
by the sheepfolds on the hillside,
if by chance you see there
the one I love the most,
tell him I suffer, grieve, and die.

Searching for my loves,
I will go among those mountains and riverbanks,
nor will I pick the flowers,
nor fear the wild beasts,
and I will pass beyond the forts and frontiers.

Question to the creatures

Oh woods and thickets,
planted by the Beloved's hand!
Oh field of greenery,

de flores esmaltado!,
decid si por vosotros ha pasado.

Respuesta de las criaturas

Mil gracias derramando
pasó por estos sotos con presura,
y, yéndolos mirando,
con sola su figura
vestidos los dejó de hermosura.

Esposo

¡Ay!, ¿quién podrá sanarme?
Acaba de entregarte ya de vero;
no quieras enviarme
de hoy más ya mensajero,
que no saben decirme lo que quiero.

Y todos cuantos vagan,
de ti me van mil gracias refiriendo,
y todos más me llagan,
y déjame muriendo
un no sé qué que quedan balbuciendo.

Mas, ¿cómo perseveras,
¡oh vida!, no viviendo donde vives,
y haciendo porque mueras
las flechas que recibes
de lo que del Amado en ti concibes?

of enameled flowers!,
tell us if he has passed by.

Response of the creatures

Spreading a thousand graces,
he passed by those groves in haste,
and gazing at them along the way,
with his countenance alone
he left them dressed in beauty.

Wife

Oh! Who will heal me!
From now on, truly,
send no more messengers
who don't know
how to tell me what I desire.

And all those who wander,
offer a thousand of your graces,
which wound me all the more
and leave me dying,
an I don't know what that they keep babbling.

But, how do you persevere,
oh life!, not living where you live,
and living so you will die
of the arrows that you receive,
which you conceive of the Beloved in you?

¿Por qué, pues, has llagado
aqueste corazón, no le sanaste?
Y pues me le has robado,
¿por qué así le dejaste,
y no tomas el robo que robaste?

Apaga mis enojos,
pues que ninguno basta a deshacellos,
y véante mis ojos,
pues eres lumbre dellos,
y solo para ti quiero tenellos.

Descubre tu presencia,
y máteme tu vista y hermosura;
mira que lo dolencia
de amor, que no se cura
sino con la presencia y la figura.

¡Oh cristalina fuente,
si en esos tus semblantes plateados
formases de repente
los ojos deseados
que tengo en mis entrañas dibujados!

¡Apártalos, Amado,
que voy de vuelo!

Esposo

Now that you have wounded
this heart, why didn't you heal it?
And because you have stolen it,
why did you leave it behind,
and not keep the thing that you stole?

Extinguish my angers,
for no one has calmed them enough,
and let my eyes see you,
for you are their flame,
it's only for you that I have eyes to see.

Reveal your presence,
may your sight and beauty kill me;
look, take note, that this ache
of love is never cured,
save by your image and presence.

Oh crystal fountain,
if on your silver surface,
suddenly you were to fashion
the desired eyes
that I've painted in my heart!

Take them away, Beloved,
soon I must be flying!

Husband

Vuélvete, paloma,
que el ciervo vulnerado
por el otero asoma
al aire de tu vuelo, y fresco toma.

Esposa

Mi Amado, las montañas,
los valles solitarios nemorosos,
las ínsulas extrañas,
los ríos sonorosos,
el silbo de los aires amorosos,

la noche sosegada
en par de los levantes del aurora,
la música callada,
la soledad sonora,
la cena que recrea y enamora.

Cazadnos las raposas,
que está ya florecida nuestra viña,
en tanto que de rosas
hacemos una piña,
y no parezca nadie en la montiña.

Detente, cierzo muerto;
ven, austro, que recuerdas los amores,
aspira por mi huerto,
y corran tus olores,
y pacerá el Amado entre las flores.

> Return, dove,
> the wounded stag
> can be seen from the hillside
> refreshed by the breeze of your flight.

Wife

> My Beloved, the mountains,
> the solitary wooded valleys,
> the unfamiliar isles,
> the sonorous rivers,
> the whispering of the beloved breezes,

> the calm night
> coupled with the rising of dawn,
> the music within silence,
> solitude sounded,
> the dinner that delights and loves.

> Let's consume the grapes
> that have blossomed on our vine;
> meanwhile, out of roses
> we will make a pine cone,
> and no one will be seen on the mountain.

> Stop, deathly northern wind,
> come, southern wind, that remembers my love,
> breathe in my orchard,
> set free its fragrances,
> so the Beloved will stroll among flowers.

¡Oh ninfas de Judea!,
en tanto que en las flores y rosales
el ámbar perfumea,
morá en los arrabales,
y no queráis tocar nuestros umbrales!

Escóndete, Carillo,
y mira con tu haz a las montañas,
y no quieras decillo;
mas mira las compañas
de la que va por ínsulas extrañas.

Esposo

A las aves ligeras,
leones, ciervos, gamos saltadores,
montes, valles, riberas,
aguas, aires, ardores
y miedos de las noches veladores:

Por las amenas liras,
y canto de serenas os conjuro
que cesen vuestras iras
y no toquéis al muro,
porque la esposa duerma más seguro.

Entrádose ha la esposa
en el ameno huerto deseado,
y a su sabor reposa,
el cuello reclinado
sobre los dulces brazos del Amado.

Oh young women of Judea!,
while amber sends its perfume
to the flowers and rose bushes,
you dwell in distant places,
and don't want to cross our thresholds.

Hide yourself, Dear,
and turn your face to the mountains,
and you don't want to confess;
but you gaze at the companions
of the woman who travels to unfamiliar isles.

Husband

To the weightless birds,
lions, deer, fallow game,
mountains, valleys, riverbanks,
waters, airs, ardors,
and fears of the nights with eyes:

Through the joyful lyre
and song of serenades I conjured you;
let your angers cease,
and don't touch the wall,
so the wife will sleep more securely.

The wife has entered
the desired and agreeable orchard,
and she rests as she wishes,
her neck reclining upon
the sweet arms of her Beloved.

Debajo del manzano,
allí conmigo fuiste desposada,
allí te di la mano,
y fuiste reparada
donde tu madre fuera violada.

Esposa

Nuestro lecho florido,
de cuevas de leones enlazado,
en púrpura tendido,
de paz edificado,
de mil escudos de oro coronado.

A zaga de tu huella
las jóvenes discurren al camino
al toque de centella,
al adobado vino,
emisiones de bálsamo divino.

En la interior bodega
de mi Amado bebí, y cuando salía
por toda aquesta vega,
ya cosa no sabía,
y el ganado perdí que antes seguía.

Allí me dió su pecho,
allí me enseñó ciencia muy sabrosa,
y yo le di de hecho
a mí, sin dejar cosa;
allí le prometí de ser su esposa.

Beneath the apple tree,
there you were married with me,
there I gave you my hand,
and you were healed
in the same place your mother was violated.

Wife

Our flowering bed,
embroidered with the caves of lions,
laid out in purple,
built upon peace,
is conferred with a thousand gold shields.

Following in your footsteps,
young women discourse on the path
at the touch of lightning,
at wine's restoration,
emissions of divine balsam.

In the inner wine cellar
I drank of my Beloved, and when I went out
to all of that meadow land
I didn't know a thing,
and I lost the cattle that I used to tend.

There he gave me his breast,
there he taught me a very delicious science,
and in truth I gave him
myself, without keeping a thing;
there I promised to be his wife.

Mi alma se ha empleado,
y todo mi caudal, en su servicio;
ya no guardo ganado,
ni ya tengo otro oficio,
que ya solo en amar es mi ejercicio.

Pues ya si en el ejido
de hoy más no fuere vista ni hallada,
diréis que me he perdido,
que andando enamorada,
me hice perdidiza, y fui ganada.

De flores y esmeraldas,
en las frescas mañanas escogidas,
haremos las guirnaldas,
en tu amor florecidas,
y en un cabello mío entretejidas.

En solo aquel cabello
que en mi cuello volar consideraste,
mirástele en mi cuello
y en él preso quedaste,
y en uno de mis ojos te llagaste.

Cuando tú me mirabas,
su gracia en mí tus ojos imprimían;
por eso me adamabas,
y en eso merecían
los míos adorar lo que en ti vían.

My soul has been possessed,
all of my wealth, in his service;
I no longer watch the cattle,
nor have any other purpose,
for love alone is my task.

So now, if in the land
I was neither seen nor found today,
you will say that I have been lost,
because, being in love,
I lost myself and I found myself.

On certain special mornings,
we will make our garlands
of emeralds and flowers
that blossomed in your love
and are woven with a strand of my hair.

You looked at the hair
on my neck, only at that strand,
and, meditating on its flight,
you stood captured by it,
and by one of my eyes you were wounded.

When you gazed at me,
your eyes impressed your grace in me;
because you loved me,
and my eyes deserved
to adore what they saw in you.

No quieras despreciarme,
que si color moreno en mí hallaste,
ya bien puedes mirarme,
después que me miraste,
que gracia y hermosura en mí dejaste.

Esposo

La blanca palomica
al arca con el ramo se ha tornado,
y ya la tortolica
al socio deseado
en las riberas verdes ha hallado.

En soledad vivía,
y en soledad ha puesto ya su nido,
y en soledad la guía
a solas su querido,
también en soledad de amor herido.

Esposa

Gocémonos, Amado,
y vámonos a ver en tu hermosura
al monte y al collado
do mana el agua pura;
entremos más adentro en la espesura.

Y luego a las subidas
cavernas de la piedra nos iremos,
que están bien escondidas,

Don't despise me,
if you find the dark spot in me,
you can still see in me,
after you have seen me,
that grace and beauty you left in me.

Husband

The little white dove
has returned to the ark with a branch,
and now the little turtle-dove
has found her desired mate
in the green riverbanks.

In solitude she lived,
and in solitude she has built her nest,
and in solitude her loved one
guides her alone,
in solitude also, wounded by love.

Wife

Let's take our delight, Beloved,
and go to gaze at your beauty
on the hill and at the heights,
where the pure water flows;
let's enter deeper into the thickets.

And then we will go
to higher caverns of stone
and there we will enter

y allí nos entraremos,
y el mosto de granadas gustaremos.

Allí me mostrarías
aquello que mi alma pretendía,
y luego me darías
allí tú, vida mía,
aquello que me diste el otro día.

El aspirar del aire,
el canto de la dulce Filomena,
el soto y su donaire,
en la noche serena
con llama que consume y no da pena.

Que nadie lo miraba,
Aminadab tampoco parecía,
y el cerco sosegaba,
y la caballería
a vista de las aguas descendía.

the most secret of places,
and delight in the juice of pomegranate.

There you will show me
what my soul desired,
and then you will give me,
there you, my life,
what the other day you gave me.

The breath of the air,
the song of the sweet nightingale,
the grove and its grace
in the serene night,
with flame that consumes and gives no sadness.

And no one looked at it;
nor did Aminadab appear,
and the calm horse ring
and the cavalry
descended within sight of the waters.

Llama de Amor Viva

Canciones del alma en la íntima comunicación de unión de amor de Dios

¡Oh llama de amor viva,
que tiernamente hieres
de mi alma en el más profundo centro!
Pues ya no eres esquiva,
acaba ya si quieres;
rompe la tela deste dulce encuentro.

¡Oh cauterio suave!
¡Oh regalada llaga!
¡Oh mano blanda! ¡Oh toque delicado,
que a vida eterna sabe,
y toda deuda paga!,
matando, muerte en vida la has trocado.

¡Oh lámparas de fuego,
en cuyos resplandores
las profundas cavernas del sentido,
que estaba oscuro y ciego,
con extraños primores
calor y luz dan junto a su querido!

¡Cuán manso y amoroso
recuerdas en mi seno,
donde secretamente solo moras;

FLAME OF LIVING LOVE

*Songs of the Soul in Intimate Communication with the
Love of God*

Oh flame of living love,
so tenderly you wound
my soul in its innermost place!
Now that you are no longer elusive,
end, if you wish,
rend the cloth of this sweet encounter.

Oh soft healing of the flesh!
Oh delicate wound!
Oh tender hand! Oh delicate touch,
that tastes of eternal life,
and pays all debt!,
killing, you have changed death to life.

Oh lamps of fire,
in whose shining
the deep caverns of sense,
that was dark and blind,
with strange exquisiteness
cast light and heat near its beloved!

How meek and loving
you awaken in my breast,
where secretly you live;

y en tu aspirar sabroso,
de bien y gloria lleno,
cuán delicadamente me enamoras!

and in your delightful breath,
full of glory and goodness,
how delicately you love me!

COPLAS DEL MISMO HECHAS SOBRE UN ÉXTASIS DE ALTA CONTEMPLACIÓN

Entréme donde no supe,
y quedéme no sabiendo,
toda sciencia trascendiendo.

Yo no supe dónde entraba,
pero, cuando allí me vi,
sin saber dónde me estaba,
grandes cosas entendí;
no diré lo que sentí,
que me quedé no sabiendo,
toda sciencia trascendiendo.

De paz y de piedad
era la sciencia perfecta,
en profunda soledad,
entendida vía recta;
era cosa tan secreta,
que me quedé balbuciendo,
toda sciencia trascendiendo.

Estaba tan embebido,
tan absorto y ajenado,
que se quedó mi sentido
de todo sentir privado,
y el espíritu dotado
de un entender no entendiendo,
toda sciencia trascendiendo.

Songs Written about an Ecstasy of High Contemplation

I entered where I didn't know,
and I remained not knowing,
going beyond all knowledge.

I didn't know where I entered,
but, there, when I saw myself,
without knowing where I was,
great things I came to know;
I will not tell what I felt,
for I remained not knowing,
going beyond all knowledge.

Of peace and mercy
was the perfect science,
in a solitude of such depth,
I knew which path was straight;
It was such a secret thing
that I continued babbling,
going beyond all knowledge.

I was so taken in,
so absorbed and estranged,
that my sense remained
apart from my private feelings;
and the spirit was gifted
with a knowing not knowing,
going beyond all knowledge.

El que allí llega de vero,
de sí mismo desfallesce;
cuanto sabía primero
mucho bajo le paresce;
y su sciencia tanto cresce,
que se queda no sabiendo,
toda sciencia trascendiendo.

Cuanto más alto se sube,
tanto menos entendía,
que es la tenebrosa nube
que a la noche esclarecía;
por eso quien la sabía
queda siempre no sabiendo,
toda sciencia trascendiendo.

Este saber no sabiendo
es de tan alto poder,
que los sabios arguyendo
jamás le pueden vencer;
que no llega su saber
a no entender entendiendo,
toda sciencia trascendiendo.

Y es de tan alta excelencia
aqueste sumo saber,
que no hay facultad ni sciencia
que le puedan emprender;
quien se supiere vencer
con un no saber sabiendo,
irá siempre trascendiendo.

Whoever arrives there truly
faints within;
of what he first knew,
much of it seems very low.
And his knowledge so increases,
that he remains unknowing,
going beyond all knowledge.

The more that one knows,
the less he understands,
that it is the darkest cloud
that elucidates the night;
therefore, the one who knows it
remains forever unknowing,
going beyond all knowledge.

And this knowing not knowing
is of such power,
the wise men could argue
and never understand
that not knowing is knowing,
going beyond all knowledge.

And of such high excellence
is this supreme knowledge,
there is no faculty or science
capable of beginning;
whoever knows is overcome
by knowing that doesn't know,
it will always go beyond.

Y si lo queréis oír,
consiste esta suma sciencia
en un subido sentir
de la divinal esencia;
es obra de su clemencia
hacer quedar no entendiendo,
toda sciencia trascendiendo.

And if you wish to hear it,
the sum of knowing consists
of a deep feeling
of the divine essence;
it's the work of its mercy
to make not knowing remain
going beyond all knowledge.

Vivo sin vivir en mí,
y de tal manera espero,
que muero porque no muero.

En mí yo no vivo ya,
y sin Dios vivir no puedo;
pues sin él y sin mí quedo,
este vivir ¿qué será?
Mil muertes se me hará,
pues mi misma vida espero,
muriendo porque no muero.

Esta vida que yo vivo
es privación de vivir;
y así, es continuo morir
hasta que viva contigo;
oye, mi Dios, lo que digo,
que esta vida no la quiero,
que muero porque no muero.

Estando absente de ti,
¿Qué vida puedo tener,
sino muerte padescer,
la mayor que nunca vi?
Lástima tengo de mí,
pues de suerte persevero,
que muero porque no muero.

Songs of the Soul that Aches to See God

I live without living in me,
and in that manner I wait,
for I die because I don't die.

I no longer live in me,
and without God I cannot live;
if without him, without me, I remain,
this living, what will it be?
A thousand deaths will befall me,
because my own life I await,
dying because I don't die.

This life that I live
is the absence of living;
and so is endless dying
until I live with you;
listen, my God, to my words,
that I don't desire this life;
I die because I don't die.

Being absent from you,
what life could I have,
but to endure death,
the worst I ever saw?
I have pity for me,
that out of luck I persist,
I die because I don't die.

El pez que del agua sale,
aun de alivio no caresce,
que en la muerte que padesce,
al fin la muerte le vale.
¿Qué muerte habrá que se iguale
a mi vivir lastimero,
pues si más vivo más muero?

Cuando me pienso aliviar
de verte en el Sacramento,
háceme más sentimiento
en no te poder gozar;
todo era para más penar,
por no verte como quiero,
y muero porque no muero.

Y si me gozo, Señor,
con esperanza de verte,
en ver que puedo perderte
se me dobla mi dolor;
viviendo en tanto pavor,
y esperando como espero,
muérome porque no muero.

Sácame de aquesta muerte,
mi Dios, y dame la vida;
no me tengas impedida
en este lazo tan fuerte;
mira que peno por verte,
y mi mal es tan entero,
que muero porque no muero.

Even the fish that leaves the water
has no lack of consolation,
because in the death it endures
death is finally worthy.
What death can ever equal
my pitiful living,
if the more I live, the more I die?

When I think to relieve myself
of seeing you in the Sacrament,
it makes me feel such grief
I can take no delight in you;
it all amounts to more pain,
from not seeing you as I desire,
and I die because I don't die.

And if I delight in myself, Lord,
with the hope of seeing you,
in seeing that I can lose you
it doubles my sorrow:
living in such dread,
and waiting as I wait,
I die because I don't die.

Take me from this death,
my God, and give me life;
don't disable me so
in this bond so powerful;
see how I grieve to see you,
and my illness is so complete,
that I die because I don't die.

Lloraré mi muerte ya
y lamentaré mi vida
en tanto que detenida
por mis pecados está.
¡Oh mi Dios!, ¿cuándo será
cuando yo diga de vero:
vivo ya porque no muero?

Now I will mourn my death,
and I will lament my life
while it's held back
by my sins.
Oh my God! When will it be
when I say in truth:
now I live because I don't die?

Otras del mismo a lo divino

Tras de un amoroso lance,
y no de esperanza falto,
volé tan alto, tan alto,
que le di a la caza alcance.

Para que yo alcance diese
a aqueste lance divino,
tanto volar me convino,
que de vista me perdiese;
y, con todo, en este trance
en el vuelo quedé falto;
mas el amor fue tan alto,
que le di a la caza alcance.

Cuando más alto subía,
deslumbróseme la vista,
y la más fuerte conquista
en escuro se hacía;
mas por ser de amor el lance
di un ciego y oscuro salto,
y fui tan alto, tan alto,
que le di a la caza alcance.

Cuanto más alto llegaba
de este lance tan subido,
tanto más bajo y rendido
y abatido me hallaba;
dije: No habrá quien alcance;
y abatíme tanto, tanto,

Other Verses to the Divine

After love's moment,
and not lacking in hope,
I flew so high, so high,
that I captured my prey.

So that I might reach
that divine moment at its height,
so fitting it was to fly,
that I passed out of your sight;
and, all in all, in this crisis
I remained lacking in flight;
but the love was so great
that I captured my prey.

When I climbed ever higher
my vision was dazzled,
and the strongest conquest
was made in the dark;
but because the moment was love,
I took a blind and dark leap
and I went so high, so high,
that I captured my prey.

The higher I rose
in this highest reaching,
the lower and stretched thin
and fallen I was;
I said: No one can overtake it;
and I was fallen so much, so much,

que fui tan alto, tan alto,
que le di a la caʒa alcance.

    Por una extraña manera
mil vuelos pasé de un vuelo,
porque esperanza de cielo
tanto alcanza cuanto espera;
esperé sólo este lance,
y en esperar no fui falto,
pues fui tan alto, tan alto,
que le di a la caʒa alcance.

that I went so high, so high,
that I captured my prey.

By a strange path
a thousand flights I passed in one flight
because in hoping for heaven
the more it's captured, the more it waits;
I awaited only this moment of love,
and I didn't fall short in waiting,
since I went so high, so high,
that I captured my prey.

Otras canciones a lo divino de Cristo y el alma

Un pastorcico solo está penado,
ajeno de placer y de contento,
y en su pastora puesto el pensamiento,
y el pecho del amor muy lastimado.

No llora por haberle amor llagado,
que no le pena verse así afligido,
aunque en el corazón está herido;
mas llora por pensar que está olvidado.

Que sólo de pensar que está olvidado
de su bella pastora, con gran pena
se deja maltratar en tierra ajena,
el pecho del amor muy lastimado.

Y dice el pastorcico: ¡Ay, desdichado
de aquel que de mi amor ha hecho ausencia,
y no quiere gozar la mi presencia,
y el pecho por su amor muy lastimado!

Y a cabo de un gran rato se ha encumbrado
sobre un árbol, do abrió sus brazos bellos,
y muerto se ha quedado, asido de ellos,
el pecho del amor muy lastimado.

OTHER SONGS TO THE DIVINITY OF CHRIST AND THE SOUL

A little shepherd alone is pained,
removed from pleasure and joy,
and his thoughts are on his shepherdess
and his heart much wounded by love.

He doesn't cry to receive love's wound
he's not hurt to see himself so stricken,
even though his heart is wounded;
he cries all the more to think he's forgotten.

Merely to think he's forgotten
by his beautiful shepherdess, with great sadness
he lets himself be mistreated in a foreign land,
his heart much wounded by love.

And the shepherd says: Oh, unhappy
the one who from my love has created absence,
and doesn't want to delight in my presence,
and my heart is much wounded by her love!

And after a long time he was raised
upon a tree, where he opened his beautiful arms,
and dead he has remained, embraced by them,
his heart much wounded by love.

CANTAR DEL ALMA QUE SE HUELGA
DE CONOCER A DIOS POR FE

Que bien sé yo la fonte que mana y corre,
    aunque es de noche.

Aquella eterna fonte está ascondida,
que bien sé yo do tiene su manida,
    aunque es de noche.

Su origen no lo sé, pues no le tiene,
mas sé que todo origen de ella viene,
    aunque es de noche.

Sé que no puede ser cosa tan bella,
y que cielos y tierra beben de ella,
    aunque es de noche.

Bien sé que suelo en ella no se halla,
y que ninguno puede vadealla,
    aunque es de noche.

Su claridad nunca es escurecida,
y sé que toda luz de ella es venida,
    aunque es de noche.

Sé ser tan caudalosas sus corrientes,
que infiernos, cielos riegan, y las gentes,
    aunque es de noche.

SONG OF THE SOUL THAT REJOICES
IN THE KNOWLEDGE OF GOD THROUGH FAITH

How well I know the fountain that springs forth and flows,
even though it is night.

    That eternal fountain is hidden,
how well I know where it has its home,
even though it is night.

    I don't know its origin, because it has none,
but I know that every origin comes from it,
even though it is night.

    I know it can't be such a beautiful thing,
and the earth and heavens drink from it,
even though it is night.

    Well I know it has no grounding,
and no one can ever cross it,
even though it is night.

    Its clarity is never obscured,
and I know all light has come from it,
even though it is night.

    I know its currents to be so deep,
that it showers the people, hells, and heavens,
even though it is night.

El corriente que nace de esta fuente,
bien sé que tan capaz y omnipotente,
aunque es de noche.

El corriente que de estas dos procede
sé que ninguna de ellas le precede,
aunque es de noche.

Aquesta eterna fonte está ascondida
en este vivo pan por darnos vida,
aunque es de noche.

Aquí se está llamando a las criaturas,
y de esta agua se hartan, aunque a escuras,
porque es de noche.

Aquesta viva fuente, que deseo,
en este pan de vida yo la veo,
aunque es de noche.

The current that springs from this fountain,
I know very well how full and strong,
    even though it is night,

The current that proceeds from these two,
I know that none of them precedes it,
    even though it is night.

This eternal fountain is hidden
in this living bread to give us life,
    even though it is night.

Here is the calling of the creatures,
and they drink to fullness, though in darkness,
    because it is night.

This living fountain that I desire,
in this bread of life I see it,
    even though it is night.

ROMANCES

I

Sobre el Evangelio "In principio
erat Verbum" acerca de la Santísima Trinidad

En el principio moraba
el Verbo, y en Dios vivía,
en quien su felicidad
infinita poseía.

El mismo Verbo Dios era,
que el principio se decía.
Él moraba en el principio,
y principio no tenía.

El era el mesmo principio;
por eso de él carecía;
el Verbo se llama Hijo,
que del principio nacía.

Hale siempre concebido,
y siempre le concebía;
dale siempre su substancia,
y siempre se la tenía.

Y así, la gloria del Hijo
es la que en el Padre había,
y toda su gloria el Padre
en el Hijo poseía.

ROMANCES

I

*Concerning the Gospel "In the Beginning
Was the Verb" with Regard to the Holy Trinity*

In the beginning resided
the Verb, and it lived in God,
in whom it possessed
its infinite happiness.

God was the Verb itself,
the beginning was spoken.
It lived in the beginning,
and it had no beginning.

It was the beginning itself;
that is why it lacked it;
the Verb is called Son,
born from the beginning.

It had always been conceived,
and always it conceived;
it gave its substance always
and always it possessed it.

And so, the glory of the Son
is what was in the Father,
and all his glory the Father
possessed in the Son.

Como amado en el amante
uno en otro residía,
y aqueste amor que los une,
en lo mismo convenía.

Con el uno y con el otro
en igualdad y valía;
tres Personas y un Amado
entre todos tres había.

Y en un amor en todas ellas
y un amante las hacía;
y el amante es el amado
en que cada qual vivía.

Que el ser que los tres poseen,
cada cual le poseía,
y cada cual de ellos ama
a la que este ser tenía.

Este ser es cada una,
y éste solo las unía
en un inefable nudo
que decir no se sabía.

Por lo cual era infinito
el amor que las unía,
porque un solo amor tres tienen,
que su esencia se decía;
que el amor, cuanto más uno,
tanto más amor hacía.

Like the beloved in the lover
one resided in the other,
and this love that joins them
coincided with the same.

With the one and with the other
in equality and worth;
three Persons and one Beloved,
the sum of them was three.

And into one love in all of them
and a lover made them;
and the lover is the beloved
in which each one lived.

For the being the three possessed,
each one possessed,
and each one of them loves
the one that this being had.

This being is each one,
and this one only joined them
in an ineffable knot
that to say was not to know.

Whereby was infinite
the love that joined them,
since three have only one love,
whose essence was spoken;
for the love, the more it was one,
the more love it created.

De la comunicación de las Tres Personas

En aquel amor inmenso
que de los dos procedía,
palabras de gran regalo
el Padre al Hijo decía,

de tan profundo deleite,
que nadie las entendía;
solo el Hijo lo gozaba,
que es a quien pertenecía.

Pero aquello que se entiende,
de esta manera decía:
«Nada me contenta, Hijo,
fuera de tu compañía.

Y si algo me contenta,
en ti mismo lo quería;
el que a ti más se parece,
a mí más satisfacía.

Y el que nada te semeja,
en mí nada hallaría;
en ti solo me he agradado,
¡oh vida de vida mía!

Eres lumbre de mi lumbre,
eres mi sabiduría;

Of the Communication of the Three Persons

In that immense love
that proceeded from the two,
words of great pleasure
the Father spoke to the Son,

of such profound delight
that no one could understand them;
only the Son enjoyed it,
the one to whom it pertained.

But what is understood,
was spoken in this way:
"Nothing pleases me, Son,
other than your company.

And if something pleases me,
I want it in you yourself;
the one who looks most like you
most satisfies me.

And the one who doesn't resemble you
will find nothing in me;
in you alone I am pleased,
oh life of my life!

You are fire of my fire,
you are my wisdom;

figura de mi substancia,
en quien bien me complacía.

Al que a ti te amare, Hijo,
a mí mismo le daría,
y el amor que yo en ti tengo,
ese mismo en él pondría,
en razón de haber amado
a quien yo tanto quería.»

3

De la Creación

—Una esposa que te ame,
mi Hijo, darte quería,
que por tu valor merezca
tener nuestra compañía,

y comer pan a una mesa,
del mismo que yo comía,
porque conozca los bienes
que en tal Hijo yo tenía,

y se congracie conmigo
de tu gracia y lozanía.
—Mucho lo agradezco, Padre,
—el Hijo le respondía—;

a la esposa que me dieres,
yo mi claridad daría,

the shape of my substance,
in whom I am well pleased.

To the one who would love you, Son,
my own self I will give him,
and the love I have for you
is the same I would place in him,
for the reason of having loved
the one I loved so much."

3

Of the Creation

—A wife to love you,
my Son, I wanted to give you,
for your worth deserves
our company,

and to eat bread at a table,
from the same table that I ate,
so she will know the blessings
that I had in such a Son,

and she will flatter me
with your grace and freshness.
—I thank you so much, Father,
—the Son responded—;

to the wife that you give me,
I will give my clarity,

para que por ella vea
cuánto mi Padre valía,

y cómo el ser que poseo,
de su ser le recibía.
Reclinarla he yo en mi brazo,
y en tu amor se abrasaría,
y con eterno deleite
tu bondad sublimaría.

4

Prosigue

—Hágase, pues —dijo el Padre,
que tu amor lo merecía.
Y en este dicho que dijo,
el mundo criado había.

Palacio para la esposa,
hecho en gran sabiduría,
el cual, en dos aposentos,
alto y bajo dividía.

El bajo de diferencias
infinitas componía;
mas el alto hermoseaba
de admirable pedrería.

Porque conozca la esposa
el Esposo que tenía,

so that by her I will see
how great is my Father's worth,

and the being that I possess,
was received from your being.
I will recline her on my arm
and in your love she would burn,
and with eternal delight
your kindness will be sublime.

4

It Continues

—Let it be, then—said the Father,
that your love has deserved it.
And with these words that he spoke,
he created the world.

A palace for the wife,
made with great wisdom,
into two rooms was divided,
upper and lower.

The lower was composed
of infinite difference;
but the higher was adorned
with marvelous jewelry.

For the wife to know
the Husband she had,

en el alto colocaba
la angélica jerarquía;

pero la natura humana
en el bajo la ponía,
por ser en su compostura
algo de menor valía.

Y aunque el ser y los lugares
de esta suerte los partía,
pero todos son un cuerpo
de la esposa que decía:

que el amor de un mismo Esposo
una esposa los hacía:
los de arriba poseían
el Esposo en alegría;

los de abajo en esperanza
de fe que les infundía,
diciéndoles que algún tiempo
Él los engrandecería,

y que aquella su bajeza
Él se la levantaría,
de manera que ninguno
ya la vituperaría.

Porque en todo semejante
Él a ellos se haría,

in the upper was placed
the angelic hierarchy;

but human nature
was put in the low place,
to be in its construction
something of less value.

And even though being and places
were divided in this way,
all exist as one in the body
of the wife, who said:

that the love of the same Husband
had made them all one wife:
the ones on high possessed
the Husband in delight;

the ones in the lower in hope
of the faith that inspired them,
telling them that one day
He will exalt them,

and that their lowliness
will be elevated by Him,
in such a way that no one
would be vengeful.

Because He will appear to them
the same in every way,

y se vendría con ellos,
y con ellos moraría;

y que Dios sería hombre,
y que el hombre Dios sería,
y trataría con ellos,
comería y bebería;

y que con ellos continuo
Él mismo se quedaría,
hasta que se consumase
este siglo que corría,

cuando se gozaran juntos
en eterna melodía;
porque Él era la cabeza
de la esposa que tenía.

A la cual todos los miembros
de los justos juntaría,
que son cuerpo de la esposa
a la cual Él tomaría

en sus brazos tiernamente,
y allí su amor le daría;
y que así juntos en uno
al Padre la llevaría,

donde del mismo deleite
que Dios goza, gozaría;

and he will come with them,
and with them he will live;

and that God will be man,
and that man will be God,
and he will live among them,
he will eat and drink;

and with them continually
He will remain himself,
until was consummated
this century that was passing,

when they would delight together
in eternal melody;
because He was the head
of the wife that he had.

Whereby, all members of the just
he will join together
in the body of the wife,
whom He will take

tenderly in his arms
and there he will give her his love,
and so, joined as one,
to the Father he will take her,

where in the same delight
that God enjoys, she will delight;

que como el Padre y el Hijo,
y el que de ellos procedía,

el uno vive en el otro;
así la esposa sería,
que dentro de Dios absorta,
vida de Dios viviría.

5

Prosigue

Con esta buena esperanza
que de arriba les venía,
el tedio de sus trabajos
más leve se les hacía;

pero la esperanza larga
y el deseo que crecía
de gozarse con su Esposo,
continuo les afligía.

Por lo cual con oraciones,
con suspiros y agonía,
con lágrimas y gemidos
le rogaban noche y día

que ya se determinase
a les dar su compañía.
Unos decían: ¡Oh, si fuese
en mi tiempo el alegría!

that as the Father and the Son,
and all that proceeded from them,

one lives in the other;
so it will be the wife,
absorbed within God,
who will live the life of God.

5

It Continues

With this good hope
that came to them from above,
the tediousness of their works
was made lighter;

but the long anticipation
and the growing desire
of delighting the husband
constantly troubled them.

So that with prayers,
with sighs and agony,
with tears and moans
they would implore him night and day

that he should now decide
to give himself to them.
Some said: Oh, if only it could be
happiness in my time!

Otros: Acaba, Señor;
al que has de enviar, envía.
Otros: Oh si ya rompieses
esos cielos, y vería

con mis ojos que bajases,
y mi llanto cesaría!
Regad, nubes de lo alto,
que la tierra lo pedía,

y ábrase ya la tierra,
que espinas nos producía,
y produzca aquella flor
con que ella florecería.

Otros decían: ¡Oh dichoso
el que en tal tiempo sería,
que merezca ver a Dios
con los ojos que tenía,

y tratarle con sus manos,
y andar en su compañía,
y gozar de los misterios
que entonces ordenaría!

6

Prosigue

En aquestos y otros ruegos
gran tiempo pasado había;

Others: Finish, Lord;
the one you are going to send, send him.
Others: Oh, if you would break open
those heavens, and I could see

with my eyes that you descend
and my weeping would cease!
Water, clouds on high,
as the earth desires,

and let the earth open now,
that produced thorns for us,
and give birth to that flower
with which it would blossom.

Others said: Oh fortunate
that one to be in such a time,
who merits seeing God
with his own eyes,

and soothe him with his hands,
and walk in his company,
and delight in the mysteries
that he will then ordain!

6

It Continues

In these and other entreaties
much time had passed;

pero en los postreros años
el fervor mucho crecía,

cuando el viejo Simeón
en deseo se encendía,
rogando a Dios que quisiese
dejalle ver este día.

Y así, el Espíritu Santo
al buen viejo respondía
que le daba su palabra
que la muerte no vería

hasta que la vida viese,
que de arriba descendía,
y que él en sus mismas manos
al mismo Dios tomaría,
y le tendría en sus brazos,
y consigo abrazaría.

7

Prosigue la Encarnación

Ya que el tiempo era llegado
en que hacerse convenía
el rescate de la esposa
que en duro yugo servía,

but in the very last years
the fervor much increased,

when the old Simeon
was enflamed with desire,
imploring God that he
be allowed to see this day.

And so, the Holy Spirit
responded to the good old man
that he gave him his word
that he would not see death

until he saw life,
that descended from above,
and with his own hands
he will touch God himself,
and hold him in his arms,
and they will embrace.

7

The Incarnation Continues

Since the time had arrived
when it seemed fitting
to rescue the wife
who had borne that hard yoke,

debajo de aquella ley
que Moisés dado le había,
el Padre con amor tierno
de esta manera decía:

Ya, ves, Hijo, que a tu esposa
a tu imagen hecho había,
en lo que a ti se parece
contigo bien convenía;

pero difiere en la carne,
que en tu simple ser no había;
en los amores perfectos
esta ley se requería,

que se haga semejante
el amante a quien quería,
que la mayor semejanza
más deleite contenía.

El cual sin duda en tu esposa
grandemente crecería
si te viere semejante
en la carne que tenía.

Mi voluntad es la tuya,
el Hijo le respondía,
y la gloria que yo tengo,
es tu voluntad ser mía.

under the law
that Moses had established,
the Father with tender love
said in this manner:

You see, Son, that your wife
was made in your image,
and insofar as she resembles you,
with you she will agree;

but she differs in the flesh,
that in your simple being you did not possess;
in those perfect loves
this law required

that the lover resemble
the one that he desires,
that the greater the resemblance
the greater the delight.

Without a doubt, in your wife
delight would blossom most grandly
if she saw that you resembled
the flesh that she had.

My will is yours,
responded the Son,
and the glory that I have
is your will to be mine.

Y a mí me conviene, Padre,
lo que tu Alteza decía,
porque por esta manera
tu bondad más se vería.

Veráse tu gran potencia,
justicia y sabiduría,
irélo a decir al mundo,
y noticia le daría

de tu belleza y dulzura
y de tu soberanía.
Iré a buscar a mi esposa,
y sobre mí tomaría

sus fatigas y trabajos,
en que tanto padescía.
Y porque ella vida tenga,
yo por ella moriría,
y sacándola del lago,
a ti te la volvería.

8

Prosigue

Entonces llamó a un arcángel,
que San Gabriel se decía,
y enviólo a una doncella
que se llamaba María,

And what your Highness said, Father,
is convenient for me
because by such means
your kindness will be revealed.

Your potency will be seen,
I will go and tell the world
of your justice and wisdom,
and I will give notice

of your beauty and sweetness
and of your dominion.
I will go to look for my wife,
and upon me I will take

her worries and labors,
in which she suffered so much.
And I would die for her
so that she will live,
and lifting her from the lake,
I will return her to you.

8

It Continues

Then he called an archangel
who was called Saint Gabriel,
and he sent him to a maiden
who bore the name of Mary,

de cuyo consentimiento
el misterio se hacía;
en la cual la Trinidad
de carne al Verbo vestía.

Y aunque tres hacen la obra,
en el uno se hacía;
y quedó el Verbo encarnado
en el vientre de María.

Y el que tenía sólo Padre,
ya también Madre tenía,
aunque no como cualquiera
que de varón concebía;

que de las entrañas de ella
él su carne recibía;
por lo cual Hijo de Dios
y del hombre se decía.

9

Del Nacimiento

Ya que era llegado el tiempo
en que de nacer había,
así como desposado
de su tálamo salía,

abrazado con su esposa,
que en sus brazos la traía,

of whose consent
the mystery was made,
in which the Trinity
dressed the Verb with flesh.

And although three make the work,
it was fashioned into one,
and the Verb remained incarnate
in the womb of Mary.

And the one who only had a Father,
now also had a Mother,
though not like any other
who had conceived with a man;

for from her womb
he received his own flesh;
whereby he was called
Son of God and of man.

9

Of the Birth

Since the time had arrived
in which he would be born,
much like a newlywed,
he set out from the bridal bed,

embracing his wife,
whom he carried in his arms,

al cual la graciosa Madre,
en un pesebre ponía,

    entre unos animales
que a la sazón allí había.
Los hombres decían cantares,
los ángeles melodía,

    festejando el desposorio
que entre tales dos había;
pero Dios en el pesebre
allí lloraba y gemía,

    que eran joyas que la esposa
al desposorio traía;
y la Madre estaba en pasmo
de que tal trueque veía:

    el llanto del hombre en Dios,
y en el hombre la alegría,
lo cual del uno y del otro
tan ajeno ser solía.

he whom the gracious Mother
had placed in a manger,

among some animals
that by chance were there.
The men sang songs,
the angels melody,

celebrating the marriage
between the two of them;
but God cried and moaned
there in the manger,

that the wife had brought
jewels to the marriage;
and the Mother was in wonder
at the exchange she witnessed:

the cry of the man in God,
and of happiness in the man,
who used to be so distant,
one from the other.

Otro del mismo que va por "Super flumina Babilonis"

Encima de las corrientes,
que en Babilonia hallaba,
allí me senté llorando,
allí la tierra regaba.

Acordándome de ti,
¡oh Sión!, a quien amaba;
era dulce tu memoria,
y con ella más lloraba.

Dejé los trajes de fiesta,
los de trabajo tomaba,
y colgué en los verdes sauces
la música que llevaba,

poniéndola en esperanza
de aquello que en ti esperaba.
Allí me hirió el amor,
y el corazón me sacaba.

Díjele que me matase,
pues de tal suerte llagaba.
Yo me metía en su fuego,
sabiendo que me abrasaba,

desculpando el avecica
que en el fuego se acababa;

By the Waters
of Babylon

By the rushing waters,
that I found in Babylon,
there I sat down weeping,
there I watered the earth.

Remembering you,
oh Zion! whom I love;
sweet was your memory,
that made me cry all the more.

I abandoned the garments of feasting,
and put on the garments of work,
and in the green willows I hung
the lyre that I carried,

placing it there in hope
of that which I hoped for in you.
There love wounded me,
and took away my heart.

I told love to kill me,
since by such fate I was wounded.
I stepped into its fire,
knowing it would burn me,

forgiving the little bird
that came to its end in the fire;

estábame en mí muriendo,
y en ti sólo respiraba.

En mí por ti me moría,
y por ti resucitaba,
que la memoria de ti
daba vida y la quitaba.

Gozábanse los extraños
entre quien cautivo estaba.
Preguntábanme cantares
de lo que en Sión cantaba:

—Canta de Sión un himno,
veamos cómo sonaba.
—Decid: ¿cómo en tierra ajena,
donde por Sión lloraba,
cantaré yo la alegría
que en Sión se me quedaba?
Echaríala en olvido
si en la ajena me gozaba.

Con mi paladar se junte
la lengua con que hablaba
si de ti yo me olvidare,
en la tierra do moraba.

Sión, por los verdes ramos
que Babilonia me daba,
de mí se olvide mi diestra,
que es lo que en ti más amaba,

I was dying inside me,
and only in you did I breathe.

For you, I died within me,
and for you I revived,
that the memory of you
took away life and returned it.

The strangers were delighted
that among them I was captive.
They asked me for the songs
that I used to sing in Zion:

—Sing a hymn of Zion,
let's see how it sounded.
—Tell me: how in a foreign land,
where I wept for Zion,
could I sing of the joy
that I left behind in Zion?
I would cast it into oblivion,
if the foreign delighted me.

May my palate be joined
to the tongue with which I speak,
if I was forgetful of you,
in the land where I resided.

Zion, by the green boughs
that Babylon gave me,
may my right hand be forgotten,
which I most loved in you,

si de ti no me acordare,
en lo que más me gozaba,
y si yo tuviere fiesta,
y sin ti la festejaba.

¡Oh hija de Babilonia,
mísera y desventurada!
Bienaventurado era
aquel en quien confiaba.

Que te ha de dar el castigo
que de tu mano llevaba;
y juntará sus pequeños
y a mí, porque en ti lloraba,
a la piedra que era Cristo,
por el cual yo te dejaba.

if I didn't remember you,
in whom I most delighted,
and if I had a feast,
and I enjoyed it without you.

Oh, daughter of Babylon,
miserable and ill-fated!
Blessed was the one
in whom I trusted,

who has given you the punishment
that you carried in your own hand;
and he will gather me up
with his little ones, because he wept for you
at the rock that was Christ,
for whom I abandoned you.

GLOSAS A LO DIVINO

Sin arrimo y con arrimo,
sin luz y a oscuras viviendo,
todo me voy consumiendo.

Mi alma está desasida
de toda cosa criada,
y sobre sí levantada,
y en una sabrosa vida,
sólo en su Dios arrimada.
Por eso ya se dirá
la cosa que más estimo,
que mi alma se ve ya
sin arrimo y con arrimo.

Y aunque tinieblas padezco
en esta vida mortal,
no es tan crecido mi mal;
porque, si de luz carezco,
tengo vida celestial;
porque el amor da tal vida,
cuando más ciego va siendo,
que tiene al alma rendida,
sin luz y a oscuras viviendo.

Hace tal obra el amor
después que le conocí,
que, si hay bien o mal en mí,
todo lo hace de un sabor,
y al alma transforma en sí;

GLOSSES ON THE DIVINE

With and without support,
without light and living in darkness,
I am consumed completely.

My soul is loosened
from everything created,
and rises within itself,
and in a sweet-tasting life
supported only by God.
That's how it will be told,
the thing that I most esteem,
that my soul is already
with and without support.

And in this mortal life,
although I suffer darkness,
my malady doesn't advance,
because, if I'm without light,
I have celestial life,
because the love of such life,
when it starts to lose its sight,
has an exhausted soul
without light and living in darkness.

Love does such work,
after a while I knew it,
that, if there is right or wrong in me,
it makes all things one taste
and becomes the soul itself;

y así, en su llama sabrosa,
la cual en mí estoy sintiendo,
apriesa, sin quedar cosa,
todo me voy consumiendo.

and so, in its delightful fire,
which I feel inside of me,
swiftly, with nothing remaining,
I am consumed completely.

GLOSA A LO DIVINO DEL MISMO AUTOR

Por toda la hermosura
nunca yo me perderé,
sino por *un no sé qué*
que se alcança por ventura.

Sabor de bien que es finito,
lo más que puede llegar
es cansar el apetito
y estragar el paladar;
y así, por toda dulzura
nunca yo me perderé,
sino por *un no sé qué*
que se halla por ventura.

El corazón generoso
nunca cura de parar
donde se puede pasar,
sino en más dificultoso;
nada le causa hartura,
y sube tanto su fe,
que gusta de *un no sé qué*
que se halla por ventura.

El que de amor adolesce,
del divino ser tocado,
tiene el gusto tan trocado
que a los gustos desfallesce;
como al que con calentura
fastidia el manjar que ve,

GLOSS ON THE DIVINE

For all that's beautiful
I will never lose myself,
except for *an I don't know what
that is reached by chance.*

The taste of goodness that is finite,
the most that it can do
is to weary the appetite
and spoil the palate;
and so for nothing sweet
will I ever lose myself,
except for *an I don't know what
that is reached by chance.*

Except in great difficulty,
the generous heart
never goes halfway
where it can continue on;
nothing can cause it misery
and its faith rises so much,
that it tastes *an I don't know what
that is reached by chance.*

Touched by the divine being,
he who suffers from love
has such an altered pleasure,
that he falls before his pleasures;
like one in a fever who
dislikes the savory dish he sees,

y apetece *un no sé qué*
que se halla por ventura.

No os maravilléis de aquesto,
que el gusto se quede tal,
porque es la causa del mal
ajena de todo el resto;
y así, toda criatura
enajenada se ve,
y gusta de *un no sé qué*
que se halla por ventura.

Que estando la voluntad
de Divinidad tocada,
no puede quedar pagada
sino con Divinidad;
mas, por ser tal su hermosura,
que sólo se ve por fe,
gústala en *un no sé qué*
que se halla por ventura.

Pues de tal enamorado,
decidme si habréis dolor,
pues que no tiene sabor
entre todo lo criado;
solo, sin forma y figura,
sin hallar arrimo y pie,
gustando allá en *un no sé qué*
que se halla por ventura.

and craves *an I don't know what
that is reached by chance.*

Don't marvel at this,
that the taste thus remains,
because it's the cause of evil,
foreign to all the rest;
and so, all creatures
are enraptured,
and taste *an I don't know what,
that is reached by chance.*

Being that the will
touched by Divinity
cannot remain satisfied
without Divinity;
but its beauty is so great,
it is glimpsed only by faith,
tasted in *an I don't know what,
that is reached by chance.*

Because of such a lover,
tell me if you will have pain,
since such love has no taste
for anything that is created;
alone, lacking form and figure,
it finds no support and standing,
tasting there *an I don't know what,
that is reached by chance.*

No penséis que el interior,
que es de mucha más valía,
halla gozo y alegría
en lo que acá da sabor;
mas sobre toda hermosura,
y lo que es y será y fue,
gusta de allá *un no sé qué*
que se halla por ventura.

Más emplea su cuidado
quien se quiere aventajar
en lo que está por ganar
que en lo que tiene ganado;
y así, para más altura,
yo siempre me inclinaré
sobre todo a *un no sé qué*
que se halla por ventura.

Por lo que por el sentido
puede acá comprehenderse,
y todo lo que entenderse,
aunque sea muy subido,
ni por gracia y hermosura
yo nunca me perderé,
sino por *un no sé qué*
que se halla por ventura.

Don't think that what is inside,
which is of greater value,
finds pleasure and happiness
in what gives taste here;
but above all beauty,
and what is, and will be, and was,
enjoys there *an I don't know what,*
that is reached by chance.

One who wishes to get ahead
should well consider
what there is to gain
more than what he has gained;
and so, to rise higher,
I will always be inclined
above all to *an I don't know what*
that is reached by chance.

For what can be comprehended
here through reason
and all that can be understood,
even though it's quite difficult,
not by grace and beauty
will I ever lose myself,
without *an I don't know what*
that is reached by chance.

DEL VERBO DIVINO

Del Verbo divino
la Virgen preñada,
viene de camino
¡si le dais posada!

OF THE DIVINE VERB

Pregnant with
the divine Verb,
the Virgin comes this way,
will you give her shelter?

Suma de la perfección

Olvido de lo criado,
memoria del Criador,
atención a lo interior
y estarse amando al Amado.

The Sum of Perfection

Forget what is created,
remember the Creator,
attention to what is inside
and loving the Beloved.

Monte de perfección

Los siguientes versillos declaran el modo de subir por la senda
al monte de perfección, y dan aviso para no ir por los dos
caminos torcidos

Para venir a gustarlo todo,
no quieras tener gusto en nada.
Para venir a saberlo todo,
no quieras saber algo en nada.
Para venir a poseerlo todo,
no quieras poseer algo en nada.
Para venir a serlo todo,
no quieras ser algo en nada.
Para venir a lo que no gustas,
has de ir por donde no gustas.
Para venir a lo que no sabes,
has de ir por donde no sabes.
Para venir a poseer lo que no posees,
has de ir por donde no posees.
Para venir a lo que no eres,
has de ir por donde no eres.
Cuando reparas en algo
dejas de arrojarte al todo.
Para venir del todo al todo,
has de dejarte del todo en todo.
Y cuando lo vengas del todo a tener,
has de tenerlo sin nada tener.

The Mount of Perfection

The following verses declare the way of ascending the path of
the mount of perfection, and advise not to enter upon the two
twisted paths

To come to take pleasure in everything,
don't want to take pleasure in nothing.
To come to know everything,
don't want to know something of nothing.
To come to possess everything,
don't want to possess something of nothing.
To come to be everything,
don't want to be something of nothing.
To come to what you don't like,
go where you don't like.
To come to what you don't know,
go where you don't know.
To come to possess what you don't possess,
go where you don't possess.
To come to what you are not,
go where you are not.
When you observe something,
stop throwing yourself at everything.
To come to the all in all,
abandon the all in all.
And when you come to have everything,
have it with nothing to have.

ACKNOWLEDGMENTS

We would like to thank our editor, Daniel Slager, for his thoughtful reading of this work. We feel privileged to have worked with him on this important project.

Born in 1962, the Mexican poet MARÍA BARANDA is a winner of major literary awards in Mexico, the Aguascalientes National Poetry Prize and the Efrain Huerta National Poetry Prize, as well as Spain's Francisco de Quevedo Prize for Ibero-American Poetry. Her books of poetry include *Narrar, Atlántica y elrústico, Avido mundo, Ficticia* (translated into English by Joshua Edwards), and *El mar insuficiente: poemas (1989-2009)*.

PAUL HOOVER is the author of the poetry volumes *Desolation: Souvenir* (2012), *Sonnet 56* (2009), *Edge and Fold* (2006) and *Poems in Spanish* (2005), which was nominated for a Bay Area Book Award. He is editor of *Postmodern American Poetry: A Norton Anthology* (1994 , 2013) and co-editor of the literary magazine, *New American Writing*. He teaches Creative Writing at San Francisco State University.

milkweed
editions

Founded as a nonprofit organization in 1980, Milkweed
Editions is an independent publisher. Our mission is to
identify, nurture and publish transformative literature, and
build an engaged community around it.

Milkweed Editions is based in Bdé Óta Othúŋwe
(Minneapolis) within Mní Sota Makhóčhe, the traditional
homeland of the Dakhóta people. Residing here since time
immemorial, Dakhóta people still call Mní Sota Makhóčhe
home, with four federally recognized Dakhóta nations and
many more Dakhóta people residing in what is now the state
of Minnesota. Due to continued legacies of colonization,
genocide, and forced removal, generations of Dakhóta people
remain disenfranchised from their traditional homeland.
Presently, Mní Sota Makhóčhe has become a refuge and home
for many Indigenous nations and peoples, including seven
federally recognized Ojibwe nations. We humbly encourage
our readers to reflect upon the historical legacies held in
the lands they occupy.

milkweed.org

Interior design by Tijqua Daiker
Typeset in Fournier

Fournier is a typeface created by the Monotype Corporation
in 1924, based on types cut in the mid-eighteenth century by
Pierre-Simon Fournier, a French typographer. The specific
cuts used as a reference for Fournier are referred to as
"St Augustin Ordinaire" in Fournier's influential *Manuel
Typographique*, published in 1764 in Paris.